Turkey Hill

A Family Vision

D1598064

4880 Lower Valley Road • Atglen, PA 19310

Other Schiffer Books on Related Subjects

Amish Arts of Lancaster County, by Patricia T. Herr
Quilting Traditions: Pieces of the Past, by Patricia T. Herr
Quilts: The Fabric of Friendship, The York County Quilt Documenta-
tion Project and the York County Heritage Trust
Fraktur: Folk Art and Family, by Corinne & Russell Earnest
*How We Lived: Everyday Furniture, Fashions, & Settings
1880-1940*, by Peter Swift Seibert

Title page image: An aerial view of Turkey Hill Dairy, c. 1960.
Above image: A view of the farm when coming up Turkey Hill, c. 1947.

Copyright © 2006 by Turkey Hill Dairy
Library of Congress Control Number: 2006925098

Designed by "Sue"
Type set in Lydian BT

ISBN: 978-0-7643-2532-8
Printed in the United States of America

Published by Schiffer Publishing, Ltd.
4880 Lower Valley Road
Atglen, PA 19310
Phone: (610) 593-1777; Fax: (610) 593-2002
E-mail: Info@schifferbooks.com

For our complete selection of fine books on this and related subjects,
please visit our website at **www.schifferbooks.com**.
You may also write for a free catalog.

This book may be purchased from the publisher.
Please try your bookstore first.

We are always looking for people to write books on new and related
subjects. If you have an idea for a book, please contact us at **proposals@
schifferbooks.com**

Schiffer Publishing's titles are available at special discounts for
bulk purchases for sales promotions or premiums. Special editions,
including personalized covers, corporate imprints, and excerpts can
be created in large quantities for special needs. For more information,
contact the publisher.

In Europe, Schiffer books are distributed by
Bushwood Books
6 Marksbury Ave.
Kew Gardens
Surrey TW9 4JF England
Phone: 44 (0) 20 8392 8585; Fax: 44 (0) 20 8392 9876
E-mail: info@bushwoodbooks.co.uk
Website: www.bushwoodbooks.co.uk

Contents

Foreword

When the Frey family immigrated to Lancaster, Pennsylvania looking for a place to worship God in peace and to escape religious persecution in Europe, they found even more than they had originally sought. The Freys were blessed by the freedom extended to them in America, and particularly in Pennsylvania. The right granted to them to own property and to work it for profit has blessed the Frey family and many others who have been associated with Turkey Hill over the years. Those blessings have increased as Turkey Hill grew, and as we met and worked with many fine employees, customers, and suppliers. Our story is unique to us, but not unique to the history of many American businesses.

Today, I recognize the treasure of the opportunity offered to us. The contributions made by our dedicated employees, as well as their loyal support and friendships, are invaluable in facing the changes and competition of the marketplace. Turkey Hill stands on the shoulders of those who leaned into the strong winds of competition, building a solid organization and a brand that many people have come to trust. This little book helps to tell their story. I hope you enjoy and benefit from it in at least some small way.

Several who have played important roles in telling this story need to be acknowledged. My thanks to Florence Herr, who authored the first draft of this history and had the initial vision for its writing. Thanks also to the editorial team of Lena Frey, Vickie Graham, Dana Huber, and Shannin Pettigrew. Thanks to my father, Emerson, and my Uncle Charles, who submitted to interviews and contributed to content in proofreading. Thanks to those who provided photos and short stories. Lastly, and very importantly, thanks to all of you who have worked for or with us, and have purchased and consumed our products.

Our deep desire is to continue to earn your loyalty by sharing with you the blessing that Turkey Hill Dairy has been for all of us.

With gratitude,

Quintin F. Frey

Quintin F. Frey,
President

Mission Statement
Our mission is to build a brand people can trust.

Vision Statement
Our vision is to earn the intense loyalty of our customers, suppliers, associates, and investors. Our products and service will go beyond what is expected. We will produce a work place that is safe, rewarding, and that offers meaningful opportunity to all associates. True to our Lancaster County heritage, we will be a trustworthy neighbor and good steward of resources. Turkey Hill will be a brand people can trust.

Enduring Principles
• Treat all people with fairness and respect.
• Practice honesty and integrity in all relationships.
• Produce and sell quality, wholesome products.
• Serve our customers as we would like to be served.

What's in a Name Like Turkey Hill?

In the soft warmth of the early spring afternoon, several canoes glided silently along the Susquehanna River. The Indian scouting party was seeking a new site for their village. The tribal wars were pushing their people farther and farther south. The land to the north was no longer able to provide the harvest necessary for their survival, and it was time to search for new hunting grounds to provide the food and furs needed for trading.

As they scouted the flat land just north of a ridge that jutted to the river's edge along the eastern shore, they saw the ground was fertile. Several older men paced off the area where the new village would be built, and the younger men scouted the surrounding area for signs of game. The river was teaming with fish and supported ducks and geese, while the land held much wildlife. Along with deer, beaver, and raccoons, they found wild turkeys on the hill to the south of the flatlands. The flock was large enough to support their people for many seasons. The Indians named this ridge south of the river plains Turkey Hill.

The first people to settle on Turkey Hill were an Indian tribe called the Susquehannock, or "people of the muddy river." They originated from what is now middle and southern New York, but slowly emigrated south as they followed the river.

The Susquehannocks were known for their farming, hunting, and fishing abilities. In the winter, they hunted and trapped animals. In the spring, after their crops were planted, they set up temporary homes to fish and gather shellfish in the lower Susquehanna River basin and Chesapeake Bay. Upon their return in the fall, they harvested maize, beans, and squash from the fields that surrounded their fortified villages.

A 2006 view of Turkey Hill Point as seen from York County. Photo by Jeffrey Hutchinson.

Captain John Smith, the founder of Jamestown, Virginia, was an early explorer in the region. When he first met the Susquehannock Indians, their imposing stature astonished him. That, however, was not enough to keep them from defeat. Through constant warring, the Susquehannocks not only lost their land, they lost their young men as well. In 1661 and 1667, smallpox epidemics further devastated their population. By 1675, the Susquehannocks were down to three hundred warriors when the Iroquois defeated them. They were taken prisoner and allowed to settle amongst the Mohawk and Oneida tribes.

Around the same time, France, England, and Spain were eagerly claiming ownership of large tracts of land in the New World, hoping to secure wealth for themselves. In 1681, as payment of debt, England's King Charles II conferred a charter of land to William Penn. It was a fifty-thousand square-mile tract of land named Penn's Woods, known today as Pennsylvania.

This drawing from an early map shows a Susquehannock Indian fort, including the longhouse dwellings. Note the different spelling used for Susquehannock. Courtesy of York County Heritage Trust.

Penn set aside the very best tract of land in Penn's Woods for his own estate, also known as a Manor. The Manor was along the Susquehanna River and included the same flat, fertile, and well watered land where the Susquehannock Indians had settled years before.

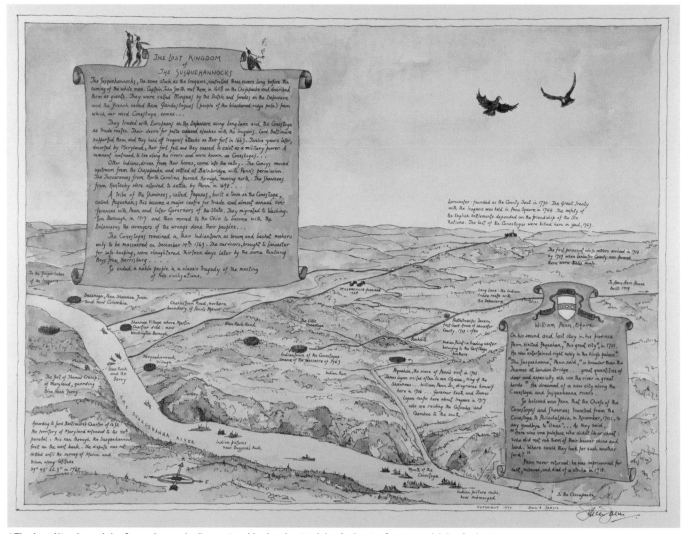

"The Lost Kingdom of the Susquehannocks," as painted by local artist John A. Jarvis. Courtesy of John A. Jarvis.

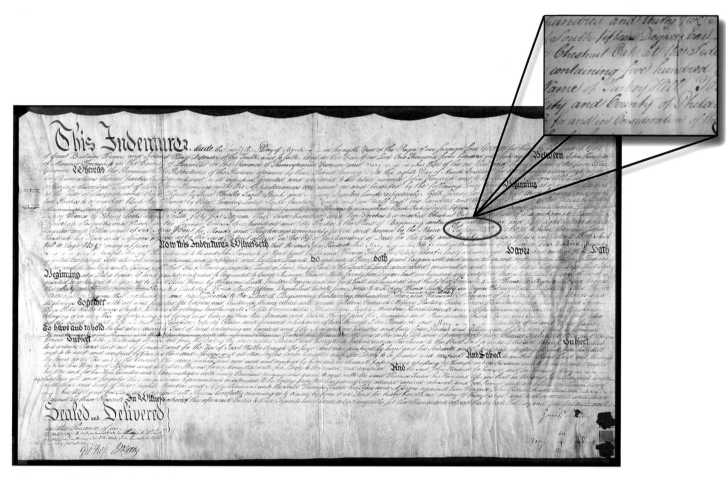

The original 1768 sheepskin deed notes the area as "Turkey Hill."

During the mid 1700s, descendents of William Penn began selling large tracts of land from the Manor. In early 1768, the portion of the Manor where Turkey Hill Dairy is located today was sold. The deed, however, was not recorded until July 1768, several months after the original sale.

The deed states:

> *Made the Twelfth Day of March in the eighth year of the Reign of our Sovereign Lord George the Third by the Grace of God of Great Britain France and Ireland King Defender of the Faith, and so forth,…Beginning at a marked Chestnut at the side of Susquehanna River thence by Jacob Wistler Jacob Schock and Adam Durslers lands respectively North seventy five Degrees East three hundred and ninety two Perches to a marked black Oak Thence by Peter Lehman's Land…containing five hundred and fifty eight Acres and a Quarter and Allowance of six Acres for Roads and Highways commonly called and known by the Name of Turkey Hill.*

The Frey family of Turkey Hill Dairy currently owns the original 1768 sheepskin deed, which notes the area as "Turkey Hill." This weathered document still contains fragments of red sealing wax affirming its authenticity and shows the creases and wrinkles acquired from many years of storage. Copies of the deed can be seen hanging throughout the Dairy today.

Life on the Farm

The farm on Turkey Hill had already been in the Frey family for over seventy years by the time Fred and Alice Frey purchased it in 1887. They worked on the farm until the early 1900s, growing tobacco as a mainstay cash crop. Fred also maintained a dairy herd and an orchard with a cider mill, and grew various crops to use for animal feed.

The farm was large enough to employ more than ten men, including Fred and Alice's son, Armor. Instead of horses and tractors, mules pulled all of the field implements. There was only one horse on the farm and it was used to pull the family buggy. Steam-powered tractors were used mainly as a stationary power source to run farm equipment using belts and pulleys. The farm buildings ranged from a large barn with a milking area in the basement to several different sized tobacco sheds, chicken coops, and smaller outbuildings, which housed the repair shop and implements.

When Fred retired in 1917, Armor took over the farm. All of Fred's hired men promptly quit, declaring they would not work for a young upstart. In time, however, a few of the men returned to work and life was back to normal on the farm. Armor and his wife, Mary, moved into the main farmhouse, while Fred and Alice relocated to their retirement home that was built just up the hill. Although officially retired, Fred continued to assist in the farm office for a number of years, as he did not consider retirement an excuse for inactivity.

Fred and Alice Frey.

There were three homes on Frey Dairy Farm. At one time, the main farmhouse stood in front of the plant, close to the top of Turkey Hill. Around 1900, a small portion of this house was separated and moved by mules across River Road and up the hill to become a second home. In 1971, the main farmhouse was moved just beyond this second home to make room for a plant expansion. The third home, Fred and Alice's retirement home, was most recently used as corporate offices for the Dairy. All three homes are still standing today and are owned by either the Dairy or a member of the Frey family.

Fred and Alice's retirement home as it stands today.

A 1920s view of the original barn built on the Frey farm in 1827.

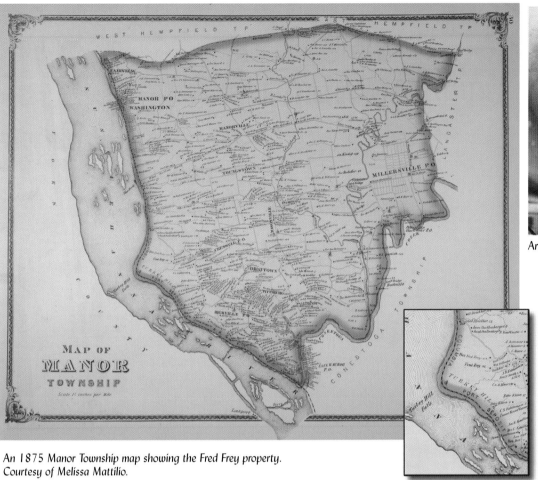

Armor Frey, a young entrepreneur.

An 1875 Manor Township map showing the Fred Frey property.
Courtesy of Melissa Mattilio.

Armor eventually decided to stop raising tobacco. His decision was based on a matter of conscience, realizing that tobacco was an unhealthy substance and against church teaching. Since tobacco had been the main cash crop for many years, Armor tried supplementing his income from the dairy herd with sheep, then later experimented with raising pigeons. Unfortunately, a few years into the Great Depression, Armor found it difficult to support both his family and hired men. By the end of 1931, he sought to generate additional income through a new venture—initiating a business that continues to sustain the Frey family today.

Armor Frey, founder of Turkey Hill Dairy, was born in 1896. As a testament to his parents, Fred and Alice, he was a man of strong convictions. His sentiments not only shaped how he farmed, but also how he treated his employees. Such a spirit was evident in 1931 when he started bottling and selling milk to support not only his family and farm, but also his hired men.

Armor did not consider himself a businessman. He was a farmer who worked hard and, as time allowed, played hard too. He enjoyed having fun with his family as well as his employees. They often played baseball in the meadow during noontime breaks and had water battles at the end of a long hot day's work. Armor loved to be outdoors, be it working in the fields, fishing in the pond, or hunting.

He and his wife, Mary, had seven children: Glenn, Emerson, Pauline, Charles, Lillian, Jay, and Eunice. Armor was the spiritual head of his family and always took them to church on the Sabbath. To make it easier on the children, Armor carried a pocketful of wintergreen candy with him. At the end of the service, when the adults joined in conversation, he passed out candy to the children as they waited patiently.

On the day Armor died in 1969, he worked all day picking corn from the field. When he sat down to rest, he said he was tired and went to bed. He passed away that night in his sleep at the age of seventy-three, leaving behind a legacy of faith and a caring spirit. Through hard work, he also left behind his business, which is still proudly called Turkey Hill Dairy today.

The Depression Years Inspire a New Venture

The Great Depression was as difficult for the people of Lancaster County as it was elsewhere. Jobs were scarce and money was tight. Emerson Frey remembers his mother telling him that during the Depression, she struggled to buy even the simplest of necessities such as a loaf of bread. Nevertheless, that did not stop his parents, Armor and Mary, from sharing what they had with others in need. When hobos stopped at the Frey farm to work for a meal and a night's lodging, the family never turned them away. There was always food left on the porch and a place to sleep in the barn. One hobo in particular, who left a special place in Emerson's heart, was an Irishman named Johnny Wood. Wood was the only hobo ever invited in to join the family at the table and share their meals. During his many visits to the farm, he entertained the Freys by singing and dancing to his favorite Irish tunes.

In the early 1930s, Armor began supplementing his income by selling milk to Penn Dairies of Lancaster. Unfortunately, the price he got for the milk did not supply an adequate income. Demonstrating the true Lancaster County spirit of ingenuity, Armor began bottling and selling milk door to door. He made this decision in part to support his farm and family, but also to support his hired help—whose livelihood depended on their farm paychecks.

Competition to sell milk in Lancaster County was fierce. Armor moved his milk by selling under the competition. If the competitor's milk was twelve cents a quart, Armor sold his for ten cents a quart. Although risky, his strategy proved to be smart, allowing him to uphold his responsibilities as a provider, farmer, and employer through the Depression.

Hobos frequently traveled in boxcars along the railway of the Susquehanna River. They often marked the gateposts of welcoming homes so the next traveler who came down the road would know it was a friendly stop.

The Armor Frey family in the 1940s.

Emerson Frey, the second oldest child of Armor and Mary, was born in 1920. He started working for his father as a boy, milking cows in the barn. After the first production building was complete, he ran the one-man bottling operation. When he and his brothers bought the Dairy in 1947, Emerson's responsibilities centered on plant and office activities.

Emerson carries on the Frey heritage, standing out as a caring, responsible, and dedicated individual, as well as a hard-driven entrepreneur. Over the course of his life, his interests have included serving in church ministries, teaching music, maintaining farms and land, and partnering with his two brothers. He also enjoyed learning about the law, an advantage when dealing with financial and corporate issues at the Dairy.

Emerson and his wife, May, had five children: Wesley, Wilson, Janna, Randall, and Quintin. After starting their family, Emerson decided to attend Messiah College in preparation for the ministry. Since there were several employees working in plant production, he was able to attend classes and still continue to run the office a couple of days a week.

While attending college, Emerson was encouraged by the Dean to change his major to music. Emerson went on to earn a degree in Music, subsequently completing his Master's from Westminster Choir College in Princeton, New Jersey. During that time, he returned to Lancaster County on weekends to work at the Dairy. After graduation, he taught music part-time at Messiah College while running the Dairy and raising his family.

Emerson and May also enjoyed gardening together and spent many years tending family garden plots. In 1989, Emerson retired from the Dairy, but continues to stay connected to the company as an advisor.

The Sons Take Charge

Despite the economic impact of the Great Depression, Armor's business continued to prosper through his bottling and selling of milk. Although the first bottles carried Armor's name, he eventually changed the name to Turkey Hill Dairy. By 1935, Armor had built Turkey Hill Dairy's first processing plant. While sons Glenn and Charles continued to work with their father on the farm, Emerson moved from milking cows to running the one-man bottling operation at the plant. Later, Emerson oversaw both the pasteurizer and the bottling line.

First processing plant, 1935.

Emerson often used creativity and skill to make the one-man bottling operation work. If he spent too much time at the pasteurizer, the collection table at the end of the bottling line would overflow and glass bottles would crash to the floor. Tired of running back and forth, Emerson developed an automatic shut-off switch on the collection table. His innovation not only improved efficiency, it also prevented a costly and unsafe situation from recurring.

Emerson Frey milks the cows.

Emerson bottles milk in the 1940s.

In 1935, President Roosevelt established the Works Progress Administration (WPA), which provided training and work for unemployed men. A team of WPA workers built an access area to an underground spring south of Columbia so people could get clear, cold spring water. They also built a stone arch access just north of the Frey farm along River Road. During a 1950s typhoid outbreak, many feared the disease would be spread through the spring. This fear resulted in both water sources being sealed. The stone arch still stands along River Road as a tribute to the work these men did.

The stone arch along River Road was inlayed with arrowheads. Although the arrowheads are no longer present, their indentations are still visible.

Glenn, Emerson, and Charles worked for their father for two dollars a week and a car. When they each turned twenty-one, Armor agreed to pay them regular wages. By the mid 1940s, however, the brothers were ready to farm their own land. Armor did not want to split up the family dairy, so as a solution, he sold the processing and retail business to these three adult sons in 1947. Armor's youngest son, Jay, was not old enough to partner with his brothers so he continued to work on the farm with his father.

Glenn Frey, the oldest son of Armor and Mary, was born in 1919. Growing up, Glenn worked with his father on the farm, either in the barn or in the field. In 1947, he went into partnership with his brothers, Emerson and Charles, to purchase the Dairy from their father.

Glenn worked with his brothers until the late 1940s when he enrolled at Elizabethtown College. In 1951, he was called to the mission field in Africa where he met and married his wife, Beth, and raised his family. While serving there, he was a pastor, administrator, architect, electrician, and carpenter.

In the early 1970s, Glenn sold his shares of Turkey Hill Dairy. After returning to the United States in 1971, he served as associate pastor at Manor Brethren in Christ Church, and then as pastor of Speedwell Heights Brethren in Christ Church. Glenn and Beth later founded the Paxton Street Home in Harrisburg, Pennsylvania, a special residency and support system for people with emotional illness needing help in daily living.

Glenn and Beth had four children: Laureen, Mary, Heather, and Eric, all of whom were born and raised in Africa. Today, Heather and her family live in the original family farmhouse within view of the Dairy. Her children are the eighth generation of Freys to live in this house.

In May 1993, Glenn and Beth were tragically killed in a car accident.

In addition to the processing facility, Turkey Hill Dairy came with two unrefrigerated trucks and two delivery routes. The brothers continued to employ Turkey Hill's two truck drivers for one hundred dollars a week, while they each took home only twenty-five dollars a week. Early on, it was apparent that Glenn, Emerson, and Charles cared for their employees just as their father had for so many years. They also cared for their community, tithing twenty percent of the Dairy's income back to God through their church and other charitable organizations.

Armor and Jay Frey on the farm.

The brothers divided the business responsibilities amongst each other. Glenn and Emerson ran the Dairy, while Charles sold and delivered the milk. Naturally, the three disagreed from time to time, but they did not fight. Each brother had his own strong points and was held accountable for solving problems in his area of expertise. When faced with differences of opinion, one of them would decide on the action to be taken and claim responsibility for the result, whether it be good or bad. When it came to major decisions, the three worked as a team to reach consensus.

The brothers' partnership led to the first major distinction between Turkey Hill Dairy and Frey Dairy Farm. Even though the businesses were separate, the family continued to share the same office space in the main farmhouse, making it easy to exchange ideas and share equipment. Emerson recalls that his first office was in the unused coal bin of the basement.

The main dairy barn, c. 1940, featured a hip gable roof. The barn was later dismantled to make room for plant expansion.

Charles Frey, the youngest brother who took over the Dairy, was born in 1926. As a young boy, he remembers getting the nickname "Chub" from a barn painter employed by Armor. Emerson claims that he and Glenn officially assigned this catchy nickname to Charles, which is still with him today.

Charles' early memories are centered around his family, on the farm, and at the Dairy. He was nine years old when the first dairy processing plant was built, and remembers riding along in the delivery truck that brought the cinder blocks from Columbia to construct the building.

Charles was only twenty-one when he, Glenn, and Emerson bought the Dairy. He was branded salesman and started selling Turkey Hill Dairy products from his truck, always looking for a chance to pick up new customers. Years later, when asked why he worked so hard, he cited his philosophy: "Decide what direction you want to go, then stick to it and work hard no matter what. It is not always easy, but you have to be true to the things you believe in. Being open to the Lord and His leading was important, but no things were sacred to me. If it was good for the company, we kept it, but when it was time to change and move on, we did that too."

Charles always maintained a sense of fun, but also had a strong work ethic like his father. He was never quick to make a decision and always willing to listen to another point of view, even if he did not agree. Dedicated to making the business grow, it was Charles' idea to manufacture ice cream commercially in the early 1950s. He later suggested opening the Turkey Hill Minit Markets in the 1960s.

Charles and his wife, Anna, had four children: Linda, Philip, Michael, and Nicholas. Like most of the Frey children, they were in and out of the Dairy, helping as they grew up. Turkey Hill was not only a place of business, but also a family hub. The Freys maintained a close community, playing and working together.

Charles retired from the Dairy in 1991, but remains an advisor. Today, he enjoys traveling, and spends extended time in Florida each year playing golf.

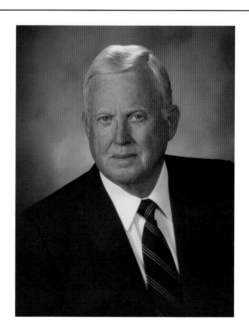

Quintin Frey is the current President of Turkey Hill Dairy. Born in 1960 to Emerson and May, he describes home to his generation of Frey children as Turkey Hill Dairy. His earliest memories include playing in and around the farm and Dairy with cousins and neighbors, building hay forts, swimming in the pond, and riding mini bikes. Over the years, he has worked in many positions in the plant and office.

Quintin and his wife, Cheryl, have four children: Derek, Ryan, Brittany, and Ethan. Like his father, Quintin decided to further his education after he was married and had children. He attended Millersville University, worked at the Dairy, and raised his family. He graduated with a degree in Economics, which prepared him for his role in leading the company. When Emerson and Charles retired, Quintin stepped in as President of Turkey Hill Dairy at the age of thirty-one. Today, Quintin's oldest son, Derek, works at the Dairy, representing the fourth generation of Freys working full time in the processing business.

Like many of the Freys before him, Quintin's faith is not a Sunday morning routine. Evident in his relationships with employees and business associates, Quintin's faith filters through his decisions all week. Although it is becoming increasingly difficult to maintain the atmosphere of a small family business, Quintin's integrity has not changed. Even in tough decisions, it remains an essential part of his character.

As both businesses prospered, Turkey Hill Dairy and Frey Dairy Farm were undeniable assets to each other. While Armor provided a good supply of high-grade milk to Turkey Hill, Turkey Hill provided an above-average supplemental income for Armor.

In 1959, both Turkey Hill Dairy and Frey Dairy Farm were incorporated. When Armor died in 1969, Jay ran the farm and the four-hundred cow dairy herd. Frey Dairy Farm remained intact, with Jay and his siblings holding equal shares. In 1985, Jay bought out all of his siblings' shares, and his family now wholly owns the farm. That same year, Dillon Companies of Hutchinson, Kansas bought Turkey Hill Dairy. Although the business is no longer family owned, it continues to be managed by Emerson's son, Quintin. With the Frey family still very much actively involved, the quality products and ethical business practices that sustained the Dairy for generations remain present today.

The Armor Frey family in the 1950s.

Milk Production

Milk Products

The business deal that Armor made with his sons in 1947 fit well into his plan. Glenn, Emerson, and Charles contracted with their father to purchase all of the milk from Frey Dairy Farm. Working together, they established a costing formula, which gave Armor the outlet he wanted to sell his premium milk at a good price.

The herd of Holstein and Guernsey cows on Frey Dairy Farm provided an ample supply of rich milk. As an experienced farmer, Armor knew that cream content depended on good cow genetics and quality feed. By balancing these key components, he successfully delivered a large quantity of milk with good butterfat measurements. Other local farmers with Holstein and Guernsey cows also sold their milk exclusively to Turkey Hill Dairy.

During Turkey Hill's early years, customers wanted the rich taste of milk with a lot of cream, so skim milk was either dumped down the drain or fed to the pigs. Contracting with farmers who provided a good rich supply of milk that produced a lot of cream was an asset to the Dairy. Cream was the mark of excellence, and prized by customers for use in their morning coffee or as an ingredient in special recipes.

Glenn, Emerson, and Charles worked hard to meet the needs of their customers. As cream-line milk shifted to homogenized milk in the 1950s, new technology was added to satisfy customer demand (see page 19). Later, cream-line milk was discontinued and the Dairy sold only homogenized milk. Cream was then sold separately in its own package.

In the 1960s, the Dairy bottled a special Golden Guernsey line of milk, along with their regular homogenized milk. In addition to being produced by Guernsey cows, which had high butterfat content, the milk was called Golden because it naturally appeared golden in color.

Holstein cows are noted for high milk production, but low butterfat content, while Guernsey cows are noted for less milk production, but high butterfat content. By blending milk from both types of cows, superior quantity and quality are produced.

Holstein cows at the Frey farm.

An early cream top bottle promotion.

Before homogenization, cream separated and rose to the top of bottled milk. Because cream was lighter than milk, it was difficult to pour without mixing it back into the milk. Some companies, including Turkey Hill Dairy, marketed a package innovation called "cream top bottles." These bottles had an expanded neck to keep the cream separate from the milk. A special spoon could easily be used to close the opening at the bottom of the neck so the cream could be poured out. Today, antique bottle collectors prize both cream top bottles and the special spoons.

Turkey Hill Dairy cream top bottles and special spoons.

Along with the Golden Guernsey line of milk, Turkey Hill Dairy offered an All-Jersey line during the 1960s and early 1970s. Knowing that farmers in southern Lancaster County had All-Jersey herds, the Dairy contracted to purchase their milk. Guaranteed to come from only one-hundred percent Jersey herds, All-Jersey Milk was promoted by Turkey Hill Dairy for its added health benefits—such as more calcium and phosphorus for strong bones and teeth, an abundance of energy-giving lactose, and extra protein.

Turkey Hill Dairy also sold chocolate milk and strawberry milk early on. While still providing an excellent source of calcium and protein, such flavored milk offers a tasty alternative. Today, the Dairy continues to produce both chocolate and strawberry milk through its "Cool Moos" line.

During the holiday season, the Dairy also provides its consumers with a great tasting egg nog. This festive blend of eggs, milk, sugar, and nutmeg is a seasonal pleasure often thought of as a dessert drink. Turkey Hill's top selling Egg Nog has been around since 1949.

Gradually, as Americans became more health conscious, the Dairy started to remove some of the butterfat from whole milk. In addition to whole milk, the regular line is now available in 2%, 1%, and fat-free varieties. Where skim milk was once a by-product of milk processing, today consumers enjoy its low-fat benefits.

Look for the Shakey Cow on "Cool Moos" products.

Milk Technology

In the 1930s, when Armor began selling raw milk, there were over two hundred small dairies doing business in Lancaster County. With so much competition, Armor realized he had to continually invest in upgrading his business to make it grow.

Initially, raw milk was bottled with a small manually operated filler that had four valves and a hand capper. Soon after the first processing plant was built, Armor replaced the manual filler with a small rotary filler. A modified version of the rotary filler is used today. While the concept has remained the same over the years, technology has changed to comply with packaging standards and to accommodate growth in production and distribution. In addition to rotary fillers, a manual bulk filler was introduced in the 1960s, and a small-pouch filler in the 1980s. Today, the bulk and pouch fillers are used for products sold to schools and hospitals.

Raw milk was cooled in the 1930s using a spring fed trough. To accommodate different size bottles, the trough was built with graduated steps. For proper cooling, bottled milk was placed in an area of the trough where the water level was at least one inch from the top. The bottles then sat in the cold-water bath until they were loaded onto the truck for delivery.

Close to the time Armor upgraded to a rotary filler, he added a pasteurization system to increase the quality and keeping time of milk. Through the use of time and temperature, pasteurization kills all of the harmful bacteria in raw milk. The first pasteurization process used at the Dairy, known as vat pasteurization, heated the milk at a low temperature for a long time. As business continued to grow, the process became more efficient. In the mid 1950s, a new pasteurizing system called High Temperature/Short Time (HTST) was introduced at the plant. True to its name, HTST increased the pasteuriza-

This 1952 version of the rotary filler used a vacuum method to fill the milk bottles mechanically, instead of manually.

High Temperature/Short Time pasteurization system.

tion temperature and decreased the pasteurization time to produce milk more efficiently. It also reduced the cooked flavor that came from the vat pasteurization process, resulting in a cleaner, purer tasting milk. HTST has stood the test of time, and still remains a critical component of the Dairy's operations today.

Around the same time that pasteurization was added, Turkey Hill Dairy invested in new technology to cool both raw and processed milk. Cooling was achieved using an ice builder, a tank with a series of tubes going through it. When the tank was filled, refrigerant was compressed in the tubes to cool the water. The ice water was then transferred to the pasteurizer or to the jacket of a storage tank where it cooled the milk. Today, similar technology is used to cool milk during the pasteurization process. The Dairy also has several single-walled storage tanks that are not jacketed. Although the milk is already cooled prior to entering these tanks, a refrigerated room keeps both the tanks and the contents cold.

During the 1950s, homogenization was introduced at the Dairy as well. Instead of letting cream separate from milk and rise to the top, the homogenizer blends the cream evenly into the milk for a smooth texture. In conjunction with the homogenizer, a separator was used to control the fat content. This machine separated the cream from the skim, and then pumped it to the appropriate tank. Through careful coordination of time and weight, the cream was manually added back into the skim to process 1%, 2%, or whole milk varieties. By the 1970s, an on-line standardization unit was installed to ensure more accuracy during the separation process. This unit, which remains in use today, tests the milk every twenty seconds. Through continuous flow, it automatically takes cream from the separator and blends it back into the milk to process the required variety.

Milk homogenizer.

Cream separator.

This 1960s Turkey Hill Dairy milk tanker was used to pick up milk from local farms.

Another breakthrough in the 1950s was the method in which milk was delivered from the farms to the Dairy. During the early years, milk was stored on the farms, then transported in ten-gallon cans by trucks. In the 1950s, this delivery system changed to tanker trucks, which were about one-third the size of today's trucks. These trucks had double jacket tanks with insulation to keep the milk cool until it arrived at the plant for processing. Aside from larger trucks and improved insulation jackets, this technology remains relatively the same today.

With the introduction of tanker trucks, the use of milk cans became almost obsolete. Although milk was no longer delivered in cans, cream continued to be delivered that way for a number of years because it was pasteurized by hand. To make heavy and light whipping creams, cans of cream were placed into a small tank. As the cream was churned by hand, a steam bath was created in the tank to simulate the pasteurization process. This labor-intensive task, which took several hours to complete, was eventually retired, and cream is now processed the same way as milk.

In the 1960s and 1970s, farmers built new milking parlors with stainless steel pipelines, which allowed the milk to be pumped directly into the storage tanks for cooling, and then into the tanker trucks for transport. To accommodate this technology, Turkey Hill Dairy built a raw receiving area. Along with the truck driver, it only took one Turkey Hill receiver to pump the milk directly from the tanker truck into the storage tanks. The tanker could be emptied and washed all in less time than it took to carry the ten-gallon cans that were once used. Not only was this process more sanitary for the milk, it was a much less labor-intensive task.

Over the years, Turkey Hill Dairy has evolved from simply selling raw milk to processing it through the use of up-to-date technology. Even though such great strides have been made, processing is still achieved through three basic components: time, temperature, and pressure.

Receiving milk and cream at Turkey Hill Dairy.

Milk Packaging

From the 1930s to the early 1960s, Turkey Hill Dairy delivered milk to its customers in various sized reusable glass bottles. Each bottle was capped with a paper lid that detailed the type of milk inside. Early bottles did not have color printing on the sides. Instead, there was a raised glass surface with the words "Armor P. Frey" and "Turkey Hill Dairy." By the 1950s, the name and location appeared on the bottles in color. Slogans and advertisements for other Turkey Hill products were later included as well.

Glass bottles contained reminders to home delivery customers to "Leave me a note for fresh Turkey Hill bread delivered to your door," or "Just a reminder we sell ..." One bottle even promotes cottage cheese sold by the Dairy. It features a picture of a cow's head that says, "I'll say . . . our cottage cheese is good."

Milk bottles showing slogans and advertisements.

Most glass bottles from the 1930s to the 1960s had a standard smooth surface, but some had a thatched raised surface as shown here.

Paper milk caps were used on glass bottles.

21

Reusable glass bottles did not provide the best means of packaging milk products sold in retail stores. By the late 1960s, Turkey Hill began to replace glass with reusable plastic gallons. The use of this reusable plastic, however, was short lived, and paperboard packages quickly became the norm. Paperboard allowed for more creativity as the Dairy could now use both color and graphics on the outside of the containers. Many may remember the "Big Chief" package that reflects how Turkey Hill got its name.

In 1994, paperboard graphics dramatically changed again. Not only did milk packages contain nutritional labels for the first time, new graphics depicting a country farm scene were added as well. The farm scene and the "Imported from Lancaster County"™ stamp helped to link milk with other Turkey Hill products, as well as with the Dairy's Lancaster County heritage.

New technology and plant expansion brought more changes to milk packaging in 1990. Milk was now offered to customers in throw-away plastic gallons. In the years since, most milk packaging has gone from paperboard to plastic. Product details are provided through self-adhesive labels, and are graphically enhanced with the identifiable Turkey Hill farm scene.

A single gallon container was not offered by Turkey Hill when milk was sold in glass and paper packaging. Customers wanting a gallon of milk had to purchase either two half gallons or the twin pack. Plastic gallon containers first appeared at the Dairy in 1990.

Reusable glass milk bottles being washed at the plant in the 1940s. Loading the bottle washer was a labor-intensive task because some bottles weighed almost a pound without milk.

Milk cartons from the 1960s to the 1990s, including the Big Chief twin pack.

Tea and Drink Production

Tea and Drink Products

As home delivery routes expanded, one goal was to offer customers more products. Initially, the drink line included only Orangeade, but it was soon expanded to include Lemonade, Breakfast Orange (a fifty percent orange juice drink with pulp), and an apricot-prune drink, known as Beep for Breakfast. Later, Iced Tea was offered as a seasonal item, but soon became a mainstay on the production calendar. As the demand for tea grew, the Dairy decided to create different flavors. Legend has it that the first flavored tea happened as an accident, when Green Spot Orangeade seeped into the Iced Tea line, and the outcome was a fifty-fifty blend of orangeade and tea. When employees tasted this mixture, they decided it was really good! In addition to the "accidental" Orange Tea, the Dairy expanded the citrus theme to include Lemon Tea as well.

Did you know Turkey Hill Iced Tea is made the cold-fashioned way? It's bottled cold, shipped cold, stored cold, and sold cold.

Turkey Hill Dairy added a research and development component to its Marketing Department in 1991. This division has been instrumental in aggressively expanding the drink line. Part of their responsibility includes experimenting with new flavors. Many flavors, such as Orange Tea, Lemon Tea, Raspberry Tea, Peach Tea, and Diet Tea, have stood the test of time and remain in the tea lineup today. Most recently, in 2005, the Dairy introduced a Regular and Diet Lime Tea and a Southern Brewed Extra Sweet Tea.

Flavored lemonades were later added to the drink line. In addition to Regular Lemonade, the Dairy offers Raspberry Lemonade, Strawberry Kiwi Lemonade, and Diet Pink Lemonade.

The next expansion in Iced Teas was the introduction of the Nature's Accents line, including herbal enhanced products with naturally inspired flavors such as Regular and Diet Green Tea, Mint with Chamomile Tea, and Blueberry Oolong Tea. In 2006, this line expanded again when Diet Green Tea Mango was added.

Pint-sized teas and drinks sold in 2006.

Over the years, Turkey Hill Dairy has expanded the distribution of refrigerated teas and drinks beyond central Pennsylvania to areas throughout the Northeast. In recent years, the Turkey Hill brand became the number one refrigerated tea in the United States, an impressive feat considering it is only sold in the Northeast portion of the country.

Tea and Drink Technology

Early on, Turkey Hill Dairy sold teas and drinks along with milk products for added variety. Since most teas and drinks are processed and bottled in much the same way as milk, adding them to the production schedule was a natural outgrowth for the Dairy. No investment of additional equipment was needed, so this was not only a sensible business move, but an easy transition as well.

In the 1950s and 1960s, the Dairy sold Big Chief Sparkle Pop sodas to customers along home delivery routes.

Tea and Drink Packaging

The evolution of tea and drink packaging reflects that of milk. The first drinks sold by Turkey Hill, such as Big Chief Sparkle Pop soda, were put into glass bottles and identified with one-color surface printing.

From the late 1960s until 1990, tea and drink products were sold in half gallon, pint, and half-pint paperboard cartons. Packages were enhanced with basic color printing and contained a minimal amount of graphics. Like milk, Turkey Hill teas and drinks also benefited from new technology in 1990. Changes at the plant allowed the Dairy to offer teas and drinks to consumers in plastic gallon containers. Other container sizes were converted from paper to plastic over the next several years as well.

A modern rotary filler used in fluid production.

A display of paperboard half-gallons and pints.

24

Pint-sized cartons featuring the first farm scene, c. 1994.

Pint tea and drink bottles converted to plastic packaging, c. 1997.

In 1994, Turkey Hill received a United States Patent for its design of the plastic half-gallon decanter. The bottle's unique shape allowed the Dairy to create a label that surrounded the body like a sleeve. Initially, the label contained a simple farm scene printed in one color. Over the years, the farm scene has changed to reflect the same one found on Turkey Hill milk and ice cream packages. Although the decanter was around for quite a while, consumer feedback prompted it to be changed to a jug with a handle in 2006.

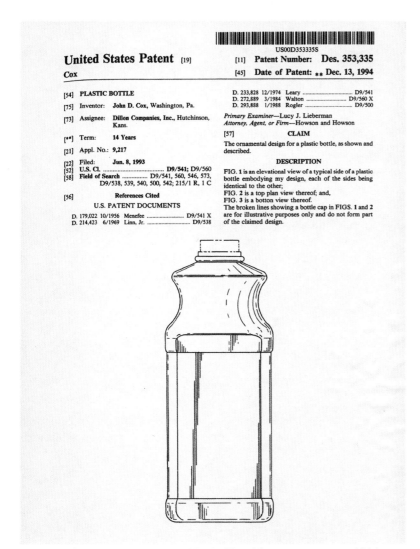

US00D353335S

United States Patent [19]

Cox

[11] Patent Number: **Des. 353,335**

[45] Date of Patent: ** Dec. 13, 1994

D. 233,828	12/1974	Leary D9/541
D. 272,889	3/1984	Walton .... D9/560 X
D. 293,888	1/1988	Rogler D9/500

[54] **PLASTIC BOTTLE**

[75] Inventor: **John D. Cox**, Washington, Pa.

[73] Assignee: **Dillon Companies, Inc.**, Hutchinson, Kans.

[**] Term: **14 Years**

[21] Appl. No.: **9,217**

[22] Filed: **Jun. 8, 1993**

[52] U.S. Cl. D9/541; D9/560

[58] Field of Search .... D9/541, 560, 546, 573, D9/538, 539, 540, 500, 542; 215/1 R, 1 C

[56] **References Cited**

U.S. PATENT DOCUMENTS

D. 179,022 10/1956 Menefee .... D9/541 X
D. 214,423 6/1969 Linn, Jr. D9/538

Primary Examiner—Lucy J. Lieberman
Attorney, Agent, or Firm—Howson and Howson

[57] **CLAIM**

The ornamental design for a plastic bottle, as shown and described.

DESCRIPTION

FIG. 1 is an elevational view of a typical side of a plastic bottle embodying my design, each of the sides being identical to the other;
FIG. 2 is a top plan view thereof; and,
FIG. 3 is a bottom view thereof.
The broken lines showing a bottle cap in FIGS. 1 and 2 are for illustrative purposes only and do not form part of the claimed design.

This Patent for the decanter was issued by the United States government in 1994.

Ice Cream Production

Ice Cream Products

When the Frey brothers first introduced ice cream at Turkey Hill Dairy, they made the same flavors their parents, Armor and Mary, made at home. The brothers multiplied their mother's recipes to produce family favorites, such as Honey Vanilla, Grape Nut, Black Raspberry, Apricot, and Peach, on a larger scale. From the beginning, they set the standard for quality by using a lot of cream, just as their father did. They never skimped on ingredients just to keep the price down. That same philosophy, which has carried through to today, is a trademark of the Turkey Hill Dairy brand.

In addition to the family favorites, Turkey Hill Dairy's other flavors included vanilla, chocolate, and ice cream made with whatever fruit was in season. It was not until 1978 that the Ice Cream Feature Flavor Program was developed. This program extended the list of regular flavors by making specialty flavors available for short periods of time throughout the year. The first two Feature Flavors were Pistachio Nut and Coffee, but the choice usually centered on fruit. Turkey Hill Dairy also offered several flavors of rippled ice cream, including Strawberry Ripple, Raspberry Ripple, and Butterscotch Ripple.

Armor and Mary Frey, c.1917.

Until Turkey Hill Dairy began distributing ice cream to supermarkets in the early 1980s, there was very little change to the regular and Feature Flavor products. Over the course of the last twenty plus years, however, Turkey Hill has aggressively introduced many new flavors and product lines to satisfy the changing palates of consumers. In 1986, the Dairy produced a line of ice milk called Turkey Hill Gourmet Lite. This line, which provided a healthy alternative to premium ice cream, was well received by the calorie conscious consumer. In 1993, changes in federal labeling laws allowed ice cream producers to reclassify ice milk as reduced fat, low-fat, or nonfat ice cream. Gourmet Lite was then classified as a reduced fat ice cream, and today it is called Light Recipe™ Ice Cream. As the trend toward lower calorie desserts continued throughout the next decade, the Dairy provided consumers with healthier options by introducing No-Sugar Added Recipe Ice Cream in low-fat and fat-free flavors.

In 1989, Turkey Hill Dairy introduced a line of Frozen Yogurt. Shortly thereafter, several new flavors of low-fat and fat-free Frozen Yogurt were added. Now, the Frozen Yogurt line also includes Limited Edition flavors such as Southern Lemon Pie and Blueberry Muffin. Although Turkey Hill is only a regional dairy, the Frozen Yogurt line is one of the top selling frozen yogurt brands in the United States, and continues to experience positive growth as more people discover the health benefits of yogurt.

A sales sheet showing ice cream packaging with the addition of Gourmet Lite and Frozen Yogurt, c. 1990.

This Frey family favorite, Vanilla made with honey and eggs, featured a bowl of ice cream on the front of the box.

26

In 1998, Turkey Hill's vision to create a line of ice cream novelties similar to its premium ice cream products in flavor and quality was realized. Beginning with a traditional Vanilla Ice Cream Sandwich, this line was later expanded to include a No Sugar Added Recipe Mint Chocolate Chip Sandwich and a Vanilla Frozen Yogurt Ice Cream Sandwich. The Double Decker, featuring a half vanilla and a half chocolate ice cream center between a vanilla and a chocolate wafer, was added as well. Through the Feature Flavor Program, a new Feature Flavor Sandwich is offered each year. Flavors have included Peanut Butter Swirl, Cookies 'n Cream, Raspberry, Southern Lemon Pie, Choco Malt Chip, and Strawberry Cheesecake. To complement ice cream sandwiches, Sundae Cones were added to the novelty line in 1999, and Chocolate Chip and Oatmeal Raisin Ice Cream Cookie Sandwiches in 2005.

Around the new millennium, when consumer palates turned to comfort foods such as high-fat super premium ice cream, Turkey Hill Dairy launched a line of ice cream known as Philadelphia Style. The creamy taste of this all-natural product is a tribute to the old-fashioned, hand-cranked ice cream made in the Philadelphia tradition. It contains no preservatives or artificial ingredients, satisfying a growing consumer desire for all natural products. Today, this line of products is available as All Natural Recipe Ice Cream.

In 2003, Turkey Hill Dairy creatively co-branded with other regional and national companies to introduce a fun new line of ice cream called Creamy Commotions®. This line incorporates miniature versions of brand name confections into Turkey Hill Dairy ice cream. Creamy Commotions® includes flavors such as Choco Malt Chip, Tastykake® Chocolate Cup Cake, and Snyder's of Hanover® Chocolate Pretzel.

As the low-carb craze hit its peak, Turkey Hill introduced CarbIQ® in 2004. This line, offering consumers premium ice cream with less carbohydrates, features Vanilla Bean, Choco Mint Chip, Chocolate and Peanut Butter Paradise flavors.

Soft serve ice cream mix, which is sold to foodservice customers, was introduced in 2004, while ice cream pies were introduced in 2005. Consumers can also purchase soft serve at local ice cream shops, stadiums, and amusement parks throughout the Turkey Hill region, while pies are available by the slice at local restaurants.

A selection of Turkey Hill Dairy products sold in the 1980s.

Capitalizing on the success of the Frozen Yogurt line, Turkey Hill Dairy created a Frozen Yogurt Smoothie in 2005. Offering consumers another healthier alternative to regular ice cream, the Smoothie combines frozen yogurt with swirls of sherbet. The variety of refreshing flavors, rather unique to the Turkey Hill Dairy brand, includes Strawberry Kiwi Passion Fruit, Peach Mango, and Orange Cream Swirl. Two of the newest flavor combinations are Green Tea Mango and Raspberry Lemonade, which are also found in the Dairy's tea and drinks.

As Turkey Hill Dairy moves forward, new products continue to be introduced to meet consumer needs. Turkey Hill Dairy's Light Recipe™ Ice Cream provides yet another example of a healthier alternative, highlighting attributes such as lower calories and fat, plus beneficial calcium. The Light Recipe™ line also offers several new regular flavors, such as Jana's® Strawberry Cheesecake, MooseTracks®, and Snyder's of Hanover® Chocolate Pretzel.

A display of Turkey Hill Dairy products available in 2006.

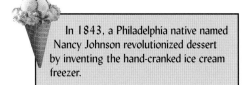

In 1843, a Philadelphia native named Nancy Johnson revolutionized dessert by inventing the hand-cranked ice cream freezer.

Ice Cream Technology
In the 1930s, ice cream was made in five-gallon hand-cranked freezers as a special treat at home. Very little ice cream was sold commercially because many people did not have a way to keep it frozen. As more homes converted to electric refrigerators with freezers, demand for ice cream increased. Although Turkey Hill continued to produce ice cream on a limited basis, growing demand led to the purchase of an electric batch freezer, which replaced the hand-cranked freezer. The batch freezer had a cylindrical freezing chamber that whipped and scraped the mix and turned it into ice cream. The mix was indirectly cooled as refrigeration was circulated through an insulated jacket surrounding the freezer. Although far less labor intensive than the hand-cranked freezer, the batch freezer still restricted how much could be made.

Older style continuous-feed freezer.

Computerized continuous-feed freezer.

In 1954, when Turkey Hill Dairy purchased an industrial continuous-feed freezer, ice cream home delivery routes were established because more ice cream could now be made. Instead of making one batch at a time, this freezer could run all day as long as mix was being supplied to it. As mix continuously entered the freezer, it was whipped with air while inside the barrel, then exited as ice cream. Instead of mixing other ingredients (such as nuts or marshmallow) into the ice cream by hand, mechanical devices did so automatically, improving both efficiency and product uniformity. A modified version of the continuous-feed freezer is still used today. Although the basic concept has not changed since the 1950s, there have been vast improvements in technology over the years. In addition to increased production and efficiency, significant changes have been made regarding setup, cleaning, and minimizing waste. Perhaps the most significant change, however, comes with computerization. Although the freezer operator's role remains critical, the computerized freezer primarily controls the production of ice cream.

One of the perks of working at the Dairy was the ice cream spout in the plant. There was a valve on the ice cream line used for flavor and consistency tests. Cones were hung on the wall near the spout, and at the end of a hard day, employees could draw themselves a nice big ice cream cone.

Ice cream was filled by hand until the 1970s, when the first automated in-line filler was introduced at the plant. Eventually, in the early 1980s, a rotary filler was added. Rotary fillers are primarily used today, but technology has changed over the years to comply with packaging standards and to accommodate growth in production and distribution. In addition to rotary fillers, Turkey Hill also has a filler used to make ice cream sandwiches and a bulk filler used to make frozen products sold primarily to restaurants and dip shops.

Filling ice cream packages by hand, c. 1956.

An automated rotary filler dispenses ice cream into packages before placing a lid on the top.

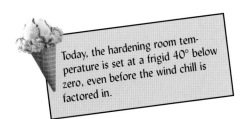

Today, the hardening room temperature is set at a frigid 40° below zero, even before the wind chill is factored in.

Emerson stacks wire baskets of ice cream in the first storage freezer.

After filling, it is important to harden the ice cream quickly to impede the formation of ice crystals and preserve its creamy texture. The first hardeners were ice and salt. Salt caused the ice to melt quickly and release the cold to harden the ice cream. Ice and salt were later replaced by Freon or ammonia coolant systems. Using this technology, Turkey Hill created a "hardening room" where the temperature was below zero. Inside this room, wire baskets containing packages of finished ice cream were manually stacked, and the ice cream was static frozen. This meant that the higher the baskets were stacked, the longer it took to freeze the ice cream. To minimize the hardening time, fans were used to create a wind chill effect. Cold air was continually circulated over the fresh ice cream so it would freeze as fast as possible.

In the 1980s, static hardening was replaced by a new system, which incorporates the use of moving trays. The trays, designed to hold different size packages, rotate the ice cream for faster hardening. To accompany this system, wire baskets were replaced by bundling, which required the installation of a shrink wrapper. This machine wraps bundles of finished ice cream packages in thick durable plastic, then applies heat to shrink the plastic to the size of the bundle. This not only increases storage capacity, it also improves distribution since there are no more wire baskets to return.

Although ice cream has been part of Turkey Hill Dairy for many years, it was produced on a small scale for several decades. When customer demands were low in the winter, ice cream production employees were often given odd jobs, such as painting, to stay busy. The real change began in the 1970s, when Turkey Hill Minit Markets experienced their fastest growth and provided an ideal outlet to make the brand more visible. However, a significant increase in ice cream production did not occur until the 1980s, when the first expansion project was launched. This project resulted in a new production room and warehouse, plus additional freezers and fillers. It also allowed for a second and third shift workforce to be put into place.

Prior to the 1990s, a bottleneck for production existed. The plant had only one pasteurizer to process all of the milk, teas, drink, and ice cream mix. In the early 1990s, however, a second pasteurizer was added—this one specifically to process ice cream mix. As a result, more mix tanks, freezers, and fillers were added, followed by a second hardening system.

Although quality ice cream making has long been a staple of the Turkey Hill brand, it has evolved from being a family favorite to a science that requires commitment, understanding, and willingness to change—all traits the Dairy has undeniably demonstrated for many years. As enhanced flavor formulations, freezing techniques, and computer automation continue to standardize ice cream production, Turkey Hill remains committed to adopting new technology as the Dairy moves forward.

Ice Cream Packaging

Ice cream packaging has progressed from simple two-color rectangular boxes to colorful, picturesque containers in many shapes and sizes. From 1954 until 1980, Turkey Hill packaged ice cream in rectangular-shaped paper boxes. Initially, these packages featured only two colors, and had either a picture of the Dairy's processing plant on the front or arrowheads around the box's perimeter. During the 1960s and 1970s, advancements in technology made it possible to create packages with pictures of ice cream flavors on the front. Later, pictures of ingredients, such as pecans, were added to the front of the packages.

The first two styles of ice cream packaging used by Turkey Hill.

In the late 1970s, the plant produced about 1,000 gallons of ice cream per day, as opposed to the nearly 100,000 gallons produced today. On the production calendar, this equates to about 25,000,000 gallons of ice cream per year, including 90,000,000 pounds of milk, 27,000,000 pounds of sugar, and 22,000,000 pounds of cream.

A selection of rectangular ice cream cartons from the 1970s.

Just as Turkey Hill Dairy started to sell ice cream through distributors, radical changes were being made to packaging. In 1981, Turkey Hill moved from packaging ice cream in boxes to packaging it in round cups with lids, featuring a window. Consumers could now see what they were purchasing and could also remove the lid, making dipping less messy. Although the same container was used for all ice cream, flavors were differentiated by the labeling on the lid. The design on these containers was minimal and had only a few colors of print.

In 1994, Turkey Hill added nutritional labels to ice cream packages to comply with new labeling laws. The Dairy used this opportunity to change the graphics as well. Instead of a small image of the farm scene in an oval, the Marketing Department expanded the scene around the circumference of the package. The flavor name was also now featured on both the cup and the lid. Other lines of ice cream began to develop an identifiable look at this time. Packages were color coded to differentiate frozen yogurt, premium ice cream, and lite ice cream. Today, color-coding is still used on packages as a means of differentiating the categories of product.

Almost twenty years after ice cream moved from a box to a round container, the shape of ice cream packaging changed again. This time, ice cream was packaged in an oval container, which, in the ice cream world, is known as a "scround." Because the scround has two relatively long, flat sides, it allows Turkey Hill to create more elaborate graphics that showcase well in the retailer's freezer. While maintaining its easy-to-dip characteristics, the scround also provides both the consumer and the retailer with a more spatially efficient package.

Color-coded round ice cream packages featuring the window on the lid, c. 1994.

In 1994, plastic "Quilt" collectible half gallons were introduced. Each package had a Lancaster County quilt design on it that changed with each new Feature Flavor. This allowed Turkey Hill to offer customers a unique collectible while simultaneously test marketing the new plastic half-gallon package.

A sample of the quilt pattern collectible package.

This display of scround packages shows the various lines of frozen products available in 2006.

Selling and Delivering Turkey Hill Products

Home Delivery Begins

For a new business with limited resources, finding new customers could be challenging. To launch his business in 1931, Armor set out in his Mitchell touring car to sell his bottled milk door to door to friends and neighbors. Through courage and determination, he successfully sold milk on his first day out, officially making him Turkey Hill Dairy's first salesman. As the lone salesman for many years, Armor's job was two-fold, both delivering milk and seeking new customers along the way. As the business grew, Armor hired deliverymen to distribute his product, while he continued to be the salesman.

Armor demonstrated the whipping capability of cream from the Dairy's milk right in his customers' kitchens. As a selling point, he poured the cream from the top of the milk bottle and demonstrated how to whip it in record time using his personal bowl and beater. Armor then turned the bowl upside down to show how light and fluffy the whipped cream was. Emerson recalls, "Dad poured and whipped the cream so fast it wasn't even funny."

Cream top bottle and beater. Armor used this beater to make whipped cream.

Ed Peters, the first driver hired by Turkey Hill Dairy, is shown with two of Armor's daughters in 1933.

Over the years Turkey Hill Dairy purchased over a dozen local dairies in order to expand their business through new delivery routes. Some of those purchased include: Home Town (Columbia), Spring Vale (West Willow), Meadow View (Mt. Joy), Goods (Rohrerstown), Harnish (New Danville), Beck's (York), Martin's (Lampeter), Wenger's Ice Cream (Mechanicsburg), Wenger's (Strasburg), Queen (Lancaster), and Moore (Lancaster).

Milk bottles from some of the dairies purchased by the Frey brothers.

Delivery routes were always service oriented. When Armor first sold milk, his customers did not have home refrigeration, thus deliveries were made seven days a week. The introduction of milk pasteurization, along with customers replacing their ice boxes with electric refrigerators, allowed Armor to cut back deliveries to three days a week.

When the Frey brothers purchased the Dairy in 1947, Charles replaced Armor as the salesman. Initially, there were only two milk delivery routes: one route went south to Safe Harbor, the other north to Columbia. Wanting to expand their customer base and sales, the brothers purchased smaller dairies throughout Lancaster County. They were not interested in the real estate or machinery from the dairies, but instead wanted the home delivery routes. Like their father, who purchased Highville, Washington Boro, and Lownesberry Dairies, the brothers acquired other dairies to grow the business and expand their delivery routes.

This 1940s photo of Turkey Hill's early fleet of home delivery trucks shows John Frey (front), Glenn Frey (middle), and Charles Frey (back). John Frey is no relation to the Turkey Hill Freys.

Milk Home Delivery

A milk deliveryman's job was never easy. Since most customers wanted fresh milk before breakfast, a deliveryman's day started at the plant between 3 a.m. and 4 a.m. After manually loading his truck with cases of bottled milk and drink, the driver went to the ice freezer. At the ice freezer, he spread crushed ice over the cases and covered them with heavy blankets to keep the product cool for delivery. Not only did he make deliveries while on route, he also collected money and obtained orders for the customer's next purchase. Upon returning to the plant between 1 p.m. and 3 p.m., the deliveryman unloaded his truck, wrote up orders for the next day, and balanced his accounts.

Regardless of the weather, deliverymen always put customer service first. During snowstorms, many deliverymen would either stay at a Frey family home or sleep in the Dairy on milk crates that were turned upside down. When necessary in the winter, the front of their trucks became plows, helping them get through snow-covered roads.

In addition to regular milk, Turkey Hill Dairy offered strawberry milk, chocolate milk, and orange juice to remain competitive. Bread, butter, and soda were eventually added to home delivery as well.

Fleet of trucks and drivers from the 1950s.

One of Turkey Hill's home deliverymen makes an early morning delivery in 1963.

LEAVE ME A NOTE FOR FRESH TURKEY HILL BREAD DELIVERED TO YOUR DOOR

Many of the Dairy's deliverymen spent their entire careers, in some cases over three decades, with the same customers on one route. As a result, lasting friendships frequently developed with the customers. Some deliverymen were invited into their customers' homes for Sunday morning breakfast. Others were asked to do odd jobs, such as dropping off a grocery list at a neighborhood grocery store, replacing a burned out fuse, or pouring milk in the cat's bowl while the customer was on vacation.

Ice Cream Home Delivery

In 1954, when Turkey Hill began making ice cream commercially, home delivered ice cream was added to the business as well. Although ice cream deliverymen did many of the same tasks as milk deliverymen, their routes were more flexible. Because ice cream stayed fresh longer than milk, it was delivered once a week from 8 a.m. to 6 p.m. Ice cream routes were laid out so the deliverymen could go into the country at the beginning of the week, and then into Lancaster City and the surrounding towns on the weekend when more people were at home. These routes could also be modified if, for instance, a holiday occurred on a weekday.

Roy Ritzman delivering ice cream in the late 1950s.

Although there were over fifteen ice cream routes by 1957, Turkey Hill Dairy hired a salesman to go door-to-door and solicit new sales. With the addition of new customers, ice cream routes continued to be added at a steady pace. By 1962, there were thirty-three ice cream routes serving Lancaster, York, and other surrounding counties.

In 1959, Turkey Hill bought D&B Frozen Specialties in Ephrata, Pennsylvania. The Dairy primarily purchased this business to acquire D&B's fleet of trucks to grow the ice cream home delivery business. However, along with the trucks came the food processing business, which included making frozen meat pies, soups, and fruit pies.

Although other dairies questioned this acquisition, Turkey Hill knew their competition was now with supermarkets. The booming economy in the 1960s led to more consumers owning automobiles as the percentage of working women grew. Supermarkets opened throughout the region, and families now conveniently shopped for their grocery needs in one place. This increased mobility, coupled with fewer stay-at-home moms, made families less dependent on home deliveries.

The new food processing business provided a way to offer customers quality products that could not be found elsewhere. These products, marketed under the name Supper Bell Foods, were first sold on ice cream home delivery routes, then later in stores. Before long, they were a welcome addition to the ice cream, soda, and snacks that were offered. Along with making their normal purchases, busy homemakers were delighted to have a quality meal delivered right to their door.

When Turkey Hill first delivered ice cream, a half-gallon of ice cream sold for $1.00.

An employee serves Supper Bell Food products at an early trade show.

37

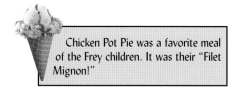

Originally, these products were made at D&B's Ephrata plant until a processing area was built at the Dairy. Later, when a larger facility was needed, a new sanitary masonry building was erected, and called the Supper Bell soup kitchen. The soup kitchen was staffed by three men, who, according to Charles, were the hardest working guys he ever employed. Even for them, however, keeping up with the demand was sometimes difficult. When the kitchen was busy, plant employees and Frey family members were often recruited to help out.

The original menu of soups included chicken noodle, beef vegetable, ham and bean, clam chowder, and oyster stew, and was later extended to include recipes that Mary Frey served to her family. Emerson worked with the head chef to develop his mother's recipes for commercial use. Chicken Pot Pie, Dutch Corn Pie, Beef Pot Pie, Macaroni and Cheese, and fruit pies made a nice selection from which Turkey Hill Dairy customers could choose.

Making dinner pies in the Supper Bell soup kitchen.

Government regulations for handling meat were strict and demanded constant attention, especially from management. With the continual growth in ice cream sales, it was apparent that ice cream provided a greater potential for growth than Supper Bell Foods. In 1984, Charles and Emerson sold Supper Bell Foods to Hanover Foods in York, Pennsylvania, and the soup kitchen was closed for good. The next year, the facility was remodeled to house the main reception area and offices for the Dairy.

One time, a soup kitchen employee drove down to the plant in a pick-up truck for some cans of milk to make Chicken Pot Pie. As he started back up the hill, the cans rolled out the back of the truck, down the hill, and into the pond. Although the cans were eventually recovered, this memory still makes for a good laugh.

Wholesale Delivery

In the early 1960s, Turkey Hill Dairy began establishing wholesale accounts with local retailers in order to reach consumers now purchasing their groceries exclusively at supermarkets. Wholesale accounts meant that Turkey Hill no longer had one on one contact with the individual consumer. Since the products were now sold through a middleman, the Dairy's salesmen faced a shift in strategy. Although the wholesaler was now Turkey Hill's customer, striving to satisfy the at-home consumer was still necessary. Because it was important that retail consumers received the same quality product as home delivery customers, each salesman had to make sure the wholesaler properly stored the products, which often required additional equipment.

LENTEN SUGGESTIONS

FISH STICKS   CRAB CAKES

FISH BURGERS   HADDOCK

IMPERIAL CRAB CAKES

MARCH, 1964

NOVELTIES
ESKIMO PIES
SANDWICHES
FUDGE POPS
ICE MILK POPS
DREAMSICLES
ICE CREAM POPS

DIABETIC QUARTS
VANILLA
CHOCOLATE
COFFEE
FRUIT FLAVOR

2 GALLON PACK
HOM MADE VANILLA
VANILLA
CHOCOLATE
FRUIT FLAVOR
NUT FLAVOR
VANILLA & CHOCOLATE

FROZEN FOODS
CHICKEN CORN SOUP
HAM & BEAN SOUP
VEGETABLE SOUP
POTATO SOUP
CLAM CHOWDER SOUP
FISH STICKS
FISH BURGERS
CRAB CAKES
IMPERIAL CRAB CAKES
HADDOCK
PEPPER CABBAGE
HAMBURG PATTIES
BEEF POT PIES
CHICKEN POT PIES
TURKEY POT PIES
CUBE VEAL STEAKS
CUBE BEEF STEAKS
MINUTE STEAKS
ORANGE JUICE, 6 OZ.
BEEF BARBECUE

1/2 GALLON FLAVORS
VANILLA
HOM MADE VANILLA
FRENCHO VANILLA
CHOCOLATE
VANILLA & CHOCOLATE
CHOCOLATE MARSHMALLOW
STRAWBERRY
BLACK RASPBERRY
PINEAPPLE
FUDGE RIPPLE
BUTTERSCOTCH RIPPLE
STRAWBERRY RIPPLE
ORANGE PINEAPPLE
BUTTER PECAN
BURNT ALMOND
NEAPOLITAN
CHERRY VANILLA
COFFEE
BUTTER CRUNCH
BUTTER CARAMEL
CHOCOLATE CHIP MINT

1/2 GALLON ICE MILK
VANILLA
CHOCOLATE & VANILLA
RASPBERRY
FUDGE RIPPLE
STRAWBERRY RIPPLE
BURNT ALMOND or BUTTER PECAN
****

REGULAR CHIPS
WAFFLE CHIPS
THIN PRETZELS
MEDIUM PRETZELS
SODA DRINK

ASK YOUR DRIVER ABOUT TURKEY HILL'S FREEZER PLAN.

MARCH FEATURE
German chocolate
ICE CREAM

PHONES: LANCASTER 8725461
          YORK   20225

A product list from 1964.

40

Various delivery trucks used in the 1980s and 1990s.

Just like home deliverymen, wholesale drivers started their day at the Dairy in the early morning hours—picking up orders and then organizing the product according to the day's deliveries. Wholesale deliverymen, however, carried milk, ice cream, and other Turkey Hill products on the same truck. Because the customer was a retail operation, products were delivered crate-by-crate instead of in small quantities. Regardless of product volume, the responsibilities of the wholesale deliveryman were similar to those of the milk and ice cream deliveryman.

Convenience Stores

It took almost twenty years to completely make the transition from home delivery to wholesale. Dairies unwilling or unable to make the change, went out of business. Eventually, the wholesale account business grew beyond small neighborhood stores to include schools, hospitals, supermarket chains, and other community vendors.

As customers changed the way they purchased products, Turkey Hill Dairy changed too. In 1967, the opening of the first Turkey Hill Minit Market provided another way to reach the Dairy's customers. New Minit Markets were built throughout the areas that were served by home delivery routes. Almost immediately, Minit Market sales were brisk, and Turkey Hill Dairy quickly assigned a representative to the account full time. The representative was responsible for acting as the company liaison between the Dairy and Minit Markets, and for ensuring the Dairy's products were delivered to the stores on time.

Initially, Turkey Hill serviced the Minit Markets the same as wholesale accounts. To become more efficient, tractor-trailer trucks eventually replaced straight trucks, allowing product to be delivered to the Minit Markets by the pallet instead of crate-by-crate. As a result, a whole new system of product handling for the drivers was created.

Turkey Hill Dairy's first fleet of trucks consisted of 1940 International panel trucks. By the 1950s, the fleet moved up to step vans, much like the bread trucks you see today. Three different models of trucks were used, including Divcos, Chevrolets, and Internationals.

Divco, Chevrolet, and International trucks.

41

Distributors

In 1981, the first tractor-trailer load of ice cream was delivered to a distributor in Philadelphia, Pennsylvania. When Abbott's Ice Cream closed their Philadelphia plant in 1980, a slot opened in city supermarkets for another ice cream brand. Turkey Hill Dairy secured that position, which took the brand into metropolitan markets throughout the Northeast. In addition to direct store deliveries, the Dairy's products were now delivered to large warehouses for distribution. Regional distributors purchased the products in large quantities, then sold them to supermarket chains and other retailers.

During this era of growth, additional sales positions were created to find new distributors of Turkey Hill ice cream and drinks. Distribution soon spread from Philadelphia to New Jersey, and then on to New York City. As Turkey Hill's ice cream reached new regions, consumer demand also allowed Turkey Hill to enter markets in surrounding regions. Products can now be found throughout New England, the Mid-Atlantic, Ohio, West Virginia, North Carolina, and Florida.

In the late 1990s, Turkey Hill began selling teas and drinks through brokers and distributors. Already familiar with the quality and value of the Dairy's ice cream, these outlets provided an opportunity to expand the distribution of teas and drinks as well.

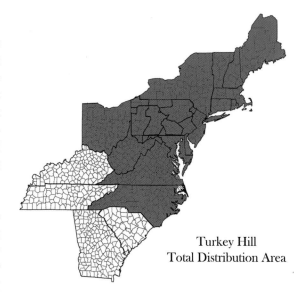

Turkey Hill
Total Distribution Area

Tractor-trailer trucks, such as this one, are used to deliver products to distributors.

Beyond United States Borders

Turkey Hill began to export ice cream in the 1990s. Initially, the Dairy only exported ice cream to Saudi Arabia, but has since expanded its international markets to include nine other countries. Turkey Hill ice cream is found in grocery stores throughout some Central American, South American, and Caribbean countries. Fans of the Dairy can now enjoy their favorite ice cream while vacationing on the sunny island of Puerto Rico.

Exporting requires the sales team to work with people who often speak a different language and live in a different culture. Because of this diversity, it is very important for the team to understand each country and its culture in order to better service the consumer.

Logistically, delivering products outside the United States is different too. Instead of products being dropped off at a warehouse, they are delivered to a domestic port. A ship then carries them to a foreign port, where they are distributed to grocery stores.

An ice cream package showing an Arabic label.

식품위생법에 의한 한글표시사항   OCS

제품명:오렌지맛 크림 스월 아이스크림
(오렌지퓨레0.468%함유)
제품유형:비유지방 아이스크림(유산균함유)
스트렙토코쿠스써모필러스, 렉토바실러스불가리쿠스유산균 함유량 400.000마리이상/1ml)
제조원:터키힐데어리사   수입원:(주)리얼에프앤비 TEL:(02) 757-2266
주 소:경기도 고양시 일산구 장항동 849 동양메이저타워 1006호 원산지:미국 용량:1.65L
원료명:탈지유(우유), 설탕, 물엿, 비유지방발효유(우유)
말토덱스트린, 오렌지퓨레, 식품첨가물:합성착색료·황색5호
영업신고번호:제2003-1263호   보관방법:영하20℃이하 냉동보관   교환장소:각 구입처
포장재질:용기내면-폴리에칠렌수지, 용기겉면-종이(폴리에칠렌코팅)
유통기한:용기 밑면에 별도표기 (일   월   년)
본 제품은 재정경제부고시 소비자 피해보상규정에 의거 보상 받을수 있음,
터키힐과 디자인은 터키힐데어리사의 상표입니다.
이미 냉동된바 있으니 해동후 재 냉동시키지 마시기 바랍니다.

Some countries, such as Korea, require labels to be translated into their native language.

Turkey Hill promotes some of their exported products in Spanish.

Annually, Turkey Hill trucks travel over 3,000,000 miles throughout the Northeast, delivering products to accounts secured by Turkey Hill sales people. The entire sales and delivery process is supported by the collective effort of many different departments, all working towards the same goal of providing prompt, friendly, and reliable service to customers, regardless of size and location.

Turkey Hill Minit Markets

The first Turkey Hill Minit Market, Store # 1, opened in June of 1967 on Columbia Avenue in Lancaster, Pennsylvania. This store is still open, welcoming customers every day.

You can still see the old style Turkey Hill Minit Markets today.

In the late 1950s and early 1960s, new technologies spurred tremendous economic growth in the United States. As more women entered the workforce, convenience became an important part of family life. Busy consumers started to choose supermarkets over corner stores because of the one-stop shopping experience that was offered.

Supermarkets also began to replace home delivery because consumers were no longer home during the day to receive their orders. As their profits fell, many home delivery services went out of business. Determined to find another way to sell Turkey Hill products, Emerson and Charles Frey set their sights on establishing a retail outlet. The brothers were familiar with a network of stores in the Philadelphia area that made it convenient for people to pick up milk, bread, and other items in a hurry. Impressed with the success of these stores, they wanted to launch a similar chain in Lancaster County.

Without experience in this area, the brothers had to find someone who could guide them through the process. They first hired a Philadelphia-based convenience store chain as a consultant, and later brought on one of the consultants as President of Turkey Hill Minit Markets.

During the first year, Emerson and Charles decided to build five stores. To further establish the Turkey Hill name, the brothers named the stores Turkey Hill Minit Markets. At the end of the first year, when they reviewed the return on their investment, it was clear they should continue building more stores. Little competition from other convenience stores in the Lancaster area, coupled with smart real estate locations, allowed the Minit Markets to experience constant growth from the very beginning.

A Turkey Hill Minit Market in 2006.

Turkey Hill Minit Market's latest logo. Look closely—it's an outline of the United States.

When Emerson decided that he did not want to co-own the Turkey Hill Minit Markets long term, he sold his shares to Charles and their partner from Philadelphia. Together, Charles and his partner formed Farmland Industries as the operating company of the Minit Markets. These stores remained a valuable asset in retailing the Dairy's milk, drinks, and ice cream.

Turkey Hill Minit Markets were the first convenience store chain to provide self-serve gasoline pumps in Pennsylvania. The first store to offer this was at the original location of Store # 8 on New Holland Avenue in 1976.

In the early 1980s, Dillon Companies of Hutchinson, Kansas were looking to purchase a convenience store chain in the mid-eastern United States. It was a lucrative market, with Pennsylvania being a central hub to major cities like Philadelphia, Baltimore, New York, and Washington. In 1985, Charles agreed to sell Turkey Hill Minit Markets to Dillon, but only if they would buy the Dairy as well. They agreed, but purchased the businesses separately. Charles withdrew from the Minit Markets completely, but remained President of Turkey Hill Dairy.

Today, Turkey Hill Minit Markets operate over two hundred and thirty convenience stores. Although increased competition in the industry and from other retailers has become a reality, the Minit Markets continue to fulfill the customer's need for convenience, value, and speed of service. Their specialty remains high quality dairy products from Turkey Hill Dairy and community involvement.

As the largest single customer of Turkey Hill, the Minit Markets have contributed greatly to the success of the Dairy. Turkey Hill likewise contributes to the success of the Minit Markets. Working as a team to reach their goals, both companies will continue to grow and succeed together into the foreseeable future.

Turkey Hill products displayed inside a Minit Market.

Marketing Turkey Hill Products

Marketing the Turkey Hill brand began much the same way that selling it did—as a one-man operation. When Armor started the business, marketing was simply selling the Dairy's products door-to-door. However, as the business grew, the marketing strategy also changed.

One of the first marketing campaigns for Turkey Hill was not for milk or ice cream, but for a drink. When Turkey Hill started selling the apricot-prune drink, home deliverymen wore pins to promote the product. The pins touted the message "Beep for Breakfast," encouraging customers to purchase this product.

Turkey Hill also geared promotions around the sale of their milk lines. Calendars were given to customers as early as the 1940s to advertise the Dairy's products, such as cream-line milk. Recipes using milk were included as well. Years later, customer brochures and other giveaways, like yardsticks, were used to promote the nutritional qualities of the All-Jersey milk line. The Dairy later introduced a giant cow to draw attention to not only All-Jersey milk, but to the Turkey Hill brand as well.

As Turkey Hill expanded into new markets, the Dairy's marketing efforts grew beyond door-to-door sales. Home delivery did not reach consumers in metropolitan areas where ice cream was sold to stores through distributors. In 1985, when Turkey Hill created a Marketing Department, employees were hired to carry out the many duties, which go beyond the development of advertising campaigns. This means the Department responds to consumer demands to develop quality products available at grocery stores or Minit Markets by handling product development and consumer relations, and supporting members of the sales team.

Product development involves market research to identify what consumers look for in new products. While some ideas never make it beyond the research stage, others help to generate premium products that consumers want to purchase. Behind the scenes, Research and Development employees within the Marketing Department continually formulate new products at the Dairy. When necessary, they also reformulate existing flavors to make Turkey Hill products even better.

Product sampling, another important part of marketing Turkey Hill products to consumers, often draws long lines of eager taste testers, such as the ones shown here in Philadelphia (1987) and the New York State Fair (2002).

This 1940 calendar was given to customers to promote milk. As an added benefit, recipes using milk were included as well.

Market research also helps the Department develop creative, appealing packaging for both new and existing products. Quality packaging is important in making a product visibly stand out to consumers in today's competitive environment.

Establishing a good consumer relationship has always been a central part of Turkey Hill. Through the Consumer Relations Call Center, the Marketing Department handles over fifteen hundred weekly calls, including questions, concerns, accolades, or suggestions. Callers are always appreciated and often receive hand-written personalized responses and coupons for Turkey Hill products.

In addition to various other day-to-day tasks handled by this Department, Marketing employees also manage giant cow appearances and attend community events. Both the giant cow and samples of Turkey Hill products are often found at community events in which Turkey Hill participates. These events provide an opportunity to meet consumers face-to-face and to get consumer feedback as well. While on location in major metropolitan areas, Turkey Hill employees are often approached by people who say, "Hey, you're that brand from Lancaster County!"

A 1940s marketing brochure.

A 1950s marketing brochure.

A 1960s marketing brochure.

Although this 2005 marketing brochure details how much Turkey Hill has grown, the look remains reminiscent of earlier brochures.

Marketing campaigns have changed dramatically from when Turkey Hill first promoted products solely through their sales force and drivers. Perhaps the company's best-known campaign to date identifies the Turkey Hill brand as being "Imported from Lancaster County™." The imported stamp was introduced in 1990 to remind consumers that Turkey Hill products come from the land of good eating, and are made by people who are honest, hard working, and capable.

In recent years, other marketing campaigns have been geared toward introducing Turkey Hill Dairy to new markets. In 2005, Turkey Hill launched a "Giant Cows Are Cool" campaign that introduced the Dairy's products in Pittsburgh and Cleveland. Through various events, the campaign brought Marketing employees in contact with consumers, while radio and television ads captured their attention by featuring talking cows. As part of this campaign, consumers in select markets also had the opportunity to win prizes through the "Cow Tipping Sweepstakes."

In 2002, the Marketing Department created rolling billboards by wrapping the fleet of delivery trucks with a farm scene.

A timeline of Turkey Hill logos.

Recently, the Dairy began to sponsor well-known regional sports teams. Perhaps you have noticed Turkey Hill as an official sponsor of a pro football or baseball team near you. Team sponsorship, which also extends to minor league baseball and pro soccer teams, allows the Marketing Department to organize promotional giveaways, ticket giveaways, and site samplings, while showing the Turkey Hill brand to new customers.

Over the years, the way consumers find out about Turkey Hill products has changed, just as marketing has grown from a one-person operation to an entire department. Although the responsibilities of marketing Turkey Hill products has expanded, the Department remains the primary contact through which the Dairy interacts with consumers.

Billboard used in Pittsburgh to promote the "Giant Cows Are Cool" campaign.

TITLE: Sovereign Ruler of Ice Cream
LENGTH: 30 SECONDS

ISCI #: ZKLM1503
FIRST AIR DATE: 6/18/2001

Music up and under throughout
ANNCR/V.O:
Say hello to Joe Wenger.

Joe's been testing for Turkey Hill Dairy ...

... going on two lifetimes now.

Last year his enthusiasm won Joe his own engraved crystal bowl ...

... and the title "Sovereign Ruler of Ice Cream."

Joe Wenger: Stupendous employee, ice cream fanatic,

and guy with cool bowl.

Turkey Hill Ice Cream. Smooth. Fresh. Inspired goodness.

Imported from Lancaster County.

"Sovereign Ruler of Ice Cream," a 2001 television commercial starring employee Joe Wenger.

52

A Herd of One, Two, Three

In 1967, Turkey Hill Dairy purchased a Jersey cow that did not resemble any other Jersey cows found on the rolling hills surrounding the Dairy. The thirteen and a half foot tall "herd of one" was made with reddish-brown fiberglass, weighed in at over thirty-five hundred pounds, and sported a set of three-foot horns. Because she was used to promote the All-Jersey line of milk, a giant milk carton was also displayed on the front of her trailer.

The first of the herd, a Jersey cow.

To name the giant cow, a contest was run asking for suggestions from schoolchildren. The contest winner suggested the name Proteina, and the newly named giant cow quickly became the company's roving ambassador. In addition to traveling to country fairs and appearing in parades, the giant cow was also used to bring attention to the opening of new Turkey Hill Minit Markets. Proteina was herded into the parking lots of new stores with the hope that people would come and investigate. She often drew customers into the store to purchase All-Jersey milk and other products.

With the horns attached to Proteina, she was too tall to go under utility lines and low underpasses. In order to travel, the horns were unscrewed and then reattached when the giant cow reached her destination.

Turkey Hill retired Proteina when the All-Jersey line of milk was discontinued. It did not take long, however, before the Dairy introduced a new cow. In 1977, Proteina was transformed from a Jersey cow to a giant black and white Holstein. At this time, her horns were permanently removed to avoid further havoc on utility lines and low underpasses.

As the market for Turkey Hill products grew beyond central Pennsylvania, the giant cow traveled longer distances. In 1985, the Turkey Hill Cow, as she became known, made her first trip outside of central Pennsylvania to Independence Square in Philadelphia for the annual "Every Day is Sundae" Festival. Because this was the first of many ice cream giveaways, the Turkey Hill milk carton on the front of the trailer was replaced with an ice cream container.

SUPER COW *Turkey Hill DAIRY*

"Where's that sassy turkey hiding?"
Protein is one of your most important food elements and you get more of it in All-Jersey milk than any other kind. Protein supplies energy. Buy All-Jersey for more protein in the yellow and red carton.
— Adv.

This is one of many Proteina comic strips printed in 1968. So, "Where's that sassy turkey hiding?"

The Turkey Hill Cow gets historical in Philadelphia.

Even though thirty years had passed since the first giant cow was built, the company that made her in 1967 is still in business. Using the original mold, this company also made the cows bought in 2000 and 2004.

Now, whenever Turkey Hill products are introduced into a new territory, the Cow can be found promoting the brand at various events. By the year 2000, her calendar had so many appearances scheduled, the Dairy decided to purchase a second giant cow. Less than five years later, a third cow was added to keep up with the demand. Although the sister cows are all the same size and shape, each has different spots. All three are kept busy attending store openings, promotional events, parades, and professional sporting events throughout the Northeast.

In 2005, the Turkey Hill Cow made her first trip overseas. The giant cow was put on a ship and sent to Puerto Rico for a few months, appearing at grocery stores carrying Turkey Hill products and at various events on the island. For the holiday season, she even sported a Santa's hat with sunglasses.

As one would expect, the Turkey Hill Cow tends to attract attention wherever she goes. This attention often results in mishaps or other experiences that make for interesting stories. The giant cow was once ticketed for speeding at seventy miles per hour. To this allegation, the driver instinctively responded, "Now officer, you know that no cow can run that fast!" Obviously, she cost Turkey Hill a little money that day. On another trip to

A herd of three.

New England, the driver recalls being pulled over by a Massachusetts state trooper, who said, "Sir, you are in no wrong, I just wanted a closer look at the passenger behind ya!" Another driver was asked to pose for a photo when the cow was traveling down a highway. Most of the time, however, kids just point and giggle, adults tend to wave, and real life cows run to the fence for a closer view.

Unfortunately, some stories are far less amusing. Because of the giant cow's height, her head was once decapitated as she went through an underpass. The cow has also been the target of vandalism, from pranksters trying to repaint her spots to more severe scrapes and cuts. She was once even a victim of a drive-by shooting in New York City. Suffering from holes in her side, she was immediately taken to the Dairy's garage, where she was patched, painted, and restored to her old self.

Although the three giant cows have never produced a drop of milk, they are assets to the Dairy, drawing attention wherever they go. After all, "Giant cows make people smile!"

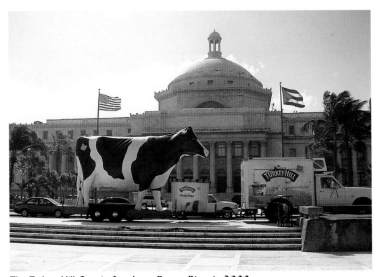

The Turkey Hill Cow in San Juan, Puerto Rico, in 2006.

Bo Vine

Bo Vine, the most knowledgeable cow in Lancaster County, first appeared at Turkey Hill Dairy in the early 1990s as a cartoon character in the company newsletter. Her role is to draw attention to articles by accompanying clever captions such as "Bo Knows Ice Cream," "Bo Knows Savings," and "Bo Knows Safe Lifting," among others.

In 1992, the Marketing team chose to create a living mascot from the Bo cartoon. After her makeover, Bo Vine literally jumped off the pages, allowing her to interact with the community. Her costume, complete with a fan and battery pack, came with a twenty-one page instruction manual. A separate manual for her animator was included as well.

In 2001, Bo was redesigned by the Marketing Department to give her a friendlier look. Contrary to the first Bo's slender appearance, the second Bo is pudgier and has more spots. The second Bo also allows her animator to navigate among the crowds of children more freely. Today, she is instantly recognizable as the loveable mascot of Turkey Hill, representing the Dairy at store openings, community events, and fundraisers.

One giant cow and Bo Vine times two. The latest version of Bo stands to the left.

Then and Now, A Part of the Community

One cannot view the history of Turkey Hill Dairy without seeing how much it is tied to the surrounding community. Living in the community near Turkey Hill Dairy brought with it many opportunities for locals to enjoy. At the same time, the community affords the Dairy ample opportunities to cultivate relationships with its customers and consumers.

Growing up near the Dairy often meant playing with the Frey children and other neighbors at Frey Dairy Farm. The grounds surrounding the Dairy offered an abundance of resources for creative and adventurous local youth. Many children enjoyed playing hide-and-seek, building forts, or playing cow pasture baseball, while the local high school basketball team often played full-court basketball in the barn, also known as "barn ball." After a long hot day, both children and adults alike cooled off in the pond, where they could go fishing, sail homemade boats, or enjoy a rowboat ride to the island in the center. In the wintertime, when the pond froze over, everyone enjoyed ice skating and keeping warm by the bonfire often lit on the island.

Families that lived several miles away in towns like Columbia or Safe Harbor were able to enjoy the benefits of living so close to both the farm and Dairy. During the 1950s and 1960s, local families often brought their children to see the cows at the farm, a visit that also included a free sample of Turkey Hill Dairy's ice cream straight off of the production line.

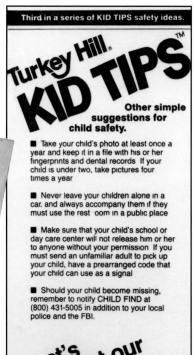

This "Garden Sunflower Quilt" was designed by Cheryl Benner exclusively for Turkey Hill Dairy and raffled off at the 1994 Lancaster Ice Cream Festival.

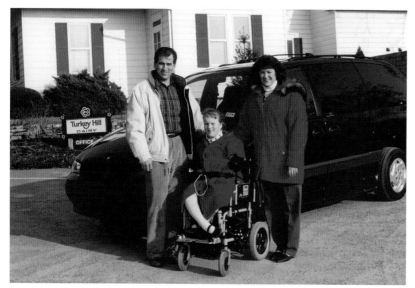

Turkey Hill Dairy's first workforce included members of the Frey family and a few others. As the business prospered, the workforce grew to include some of the same local children that once enjoyed playing at the farm. As the children became teenagers, they often took summer jobs at Turkey Hill, later becoming permanent employees. The workforce eventually reached out into the neighboring towns of Columbia, Millersville, and Lancaster. Today, most employees travel from Lancaster County and eastern York County each day to come to work. Employees also include off-site sales representatives from surrounding states, and people who have immigrated to the United States from Mexico, Puerto Rico, South America, and Africa. Because Turkey Hill Dairy employees have family ties in many parts of the world, the Turkey Hill community now extends well beyond local roots.

Turkey Hill reaches out to a fellow employee by helping him raise funds to purchase a handicapped-accessible van to transport his daughter.

The ties binding the Dairy and its employees to the community have always fostered benevolent giving. Many employees actively participate in neighborhood organizations. Some employees volunteer at local fire companies, emergency rescue units, or disaster relief organizations, while others donate their time by working with scout troops, sports teams, schools, churches, and other non-profit organizations. As a show of support, Turkey Hill often assists these organizations with fund raising events such as festivals and dinners.

The annual five-kilometer Country Classic race, involving many Turkey Hill employees, benefits local organizations.

The Dairy also sponsors many events that benefit communities where Turkey Hill products are sold. For many years, the Dairy sponsored Lancaster's Ice Cream Festival, which provided funds for the Lancaster County Library System. Thousands of people attended the annual event in July to indulge in all-you-can-eat Turkey Hill ice cream and drinks, listen to music, and take part in activities such as the ice cream stacking contest. Volunteers from Turkey Hill Dairy and the Library System set up and staffed the ice cream and drink stations throughout the day.

Turkey Hill Dairy also sponsors events outside of Lancaster County. Every July, Turkey Hill sponsors the Rockwood Foundation's Ice Cream Festival in Newark, Delaware. Annually, this weekend event draws in over seventy thousand people, who stroll through Rockwood's beautifully manicured grounds, tour the magnificent old mansion, listen to music, and watch fireworks, all while enjoying Turkey Hill ice cream. The proceeds from the festival are then used to refurbish the mansion and grounds, which are open free of charge to the public for meetings, picnics, and Sunday afternoon strolls. In 2005, with the help of these proceeds, Rockwood Foundation opened a new eleven-thousand square-foot Visitor's Center.

This mural, depicting the relationship between Lancaster County Libraries and Turkey Hill Dairy, can be seen in the Lancaster City Library.

59

Every year, Turkey Hill Dairy sponsors and contributes to over eight hundred charitable events throughout the region, aiding organizations such as Lancaster County schools, Whitaker Center, Sertoma Club, Lancaster County Hospice, Make-a-Wish Foundation, National Multiple Sclerosis Society, New Jersey Special Olympics, and the West Springfield Boys and Girls Club, among many others.

Over the course of the last seventy-five years, the Turkey Hill community has grown from those that lived within walking distance of the Dairy to communities throughout the Northeast. The company's philosophy, to build a brand people can trust, has not changed. Regardless of how far the community spreads, Turkey Hill remains committed to making meaningful contributions to the employees and the communities that have supported the company since 1931.

This "Good Ole' Farmlife" cow was designed by Tammi A. Rodman exclusively for Turkey Hill Dairy. It was part of the Harrisburg Cow Parade in 2004.

Romans 12:11 Paraphrased for Business

The following edition of Romans 12:11 was paraphrased by Emerson, and used as a standard to run his business, as well as his life. It set the core values for Turkey Hill Dairy while he and Charles were in charge.

1. Work hard at your business, but keep a proper balance between your fervor for it and the Lord's business, which you are also doing.

2. The hope of success spurs you hopefully on, but watch out, there will be many times when you lose money, so pray continually.

3. This formula permits you to have money to give to people in need, and to entertain others in your home and in your church.

4. Bless those who levy taxes and controls, those who take your customers, your market, or your money. Don't get angry about it.

5. Be happy when the other fellow is successful. Be sympathetic with those who are having a hard time of it.

6. Don't get high-minded and stuck-up when you succeed, but act just as though you had failed and were poor. Don't think your success was all because of you.

7. Don't try to beat the "sharpie" salesman or businessman because he pulled a fast deal on you. Let your dealing have an honest ring to your employees, your customers, and your fellow businessmen.

8. Some customers you can never satisfy, and some inspectors you can never please, but keep trying without getting huffy.

9. Dear fellow businessmen and women, don't think you must win every time. If you lose, don't try to make it up on the next deal. The Lord will take care of those characters.

10. Instead, do him a good turn; that will really roast him out.

11. Don't let evil cause you to fail; let good make you successful.

An aerial view of Turkey Hill Dairy in 2005.

Acknowledgments

Trademarks

Moose Tracks® and Denali® are registered trademarks of Denali Flavors, Inc. Explore www.Moosetracks.com.

Jana's® is a registered trademark of Jana's Classic, Inc.

The Snyders of Hanover trademark and trade dress are used under license.

Tastykake®, KandyKakes®, and Oatmeal Raisin Snak Bar® are registered trademarks of the Tasty Baking Company.

Photography

Product photography by Jeffrey Hutchinson, Hutch Graphics.

Contributors

Heather Abbato
Mike Arment
Jim Bolin
Rae Lynn Callahan
Dave Canter
John Cox
Jerry Estes
Derek Frey
Elisa Gochnauer
Larry Ibach
Nancy Jenkins
Samantha O'Hara
Dick Pellman
Ernie Pinckney
Brian Ressler
Erin Dimitriou-Smith
Turkey Hill Dairy Marketing Department